NORTH YORKSHIRE
COASTAL VILLAGES
THEN & NOW

IN COLOUR

COLIN WATERS

The
History
Press

First published in 2012

The History Press
The Mill, Brimscombe Port
Stroud, Gloucestershire, GL5 2QG
www.thehistorypress.co.uk

British Library Cataloguing in Publication Data.
A catalogue record for this book is available from the British Library.

ISBN 978 0 7524 6791 7

Typesetting and origination by The History Press
Printed in India.
Manufacturing managed by Jellyfish Print Solutions Ltd

CONTENTS

ACKNOWLEDGEMENTS

Though the majority of the pictures within this book are from the author's collection, gratitude must also be extended to Susan McGill, Raymond Grey and Mrs V. Brown for supplying additional images and old postcards. Thanks must also go to the original unknown photographers and artists of old who captured these fascinating village scenes as they were in their own lifetime. Appreciation must also be extended to The History Press's regional history editor Jessica Andrews and her team, for their ever friendly help and assistance during the compilation of this book.

ABOUT THE AUTHOR

Colin Waters is a writer, researcher and social historian and has contributed to radio, television, newspapers and national magazines. He was the founder and former director and president of Whitby Archives & Heritage Centre

INTRODUCTION

The villages featured in this book are all to be found on a scenic route stretching between Marske and Scalby Mills. Thanks to confusing boundary changes, the task of what to include has not been easy. As an example, Staithes near Whitby is considered to be both in Yorkshire and Cleveland. Confusingly, its postal address is Saltburn and, to complicate matters further, it has a Teesside postcode.

Only places considered truly 'seaside' villages are included. Others such as Hinderwell, Lythe and Cloughton are not. Even so they form part of the route between Marske and Scalby Mills that can easily be travelled by car (or public transport) in one day and will provide interesting stop-off points for anyone wishing to break their journey.

The starting point is Marske, which was once a fishing village but is rapidly becoming a small town. Conversely, Skinningrove, formerly an industrial centre, is now a quiet residential village with its own mining museum. Picturesque Staithes is famous for its quaint harbour, winding streets and maze of alleyways where the house in which Captain James Cook lived stands only a short walk from the museum that commemorates his life.

Despite being off the beaten track, Port Mulgrave has become a magnet for naturalists and walkers. Its once busy harbour is now barely discernable. Nearby Runswick is located on two levels. Part of it remains in a rural setting at the top of the cliffs with the remainder of the village clustering around the dramatic sweeping bay below.

A winding country lane with spectacular panoramic maritime views leads to Kettleness. A Roman signal station stood nearby and a rough path leads to the shore below. The village was once much larger but much of it slipped slowly into the sea one dark stormy night.

At Sandsend and East Row, the sometimes sea-washed roadway briefly skirts the North Sea. From here miles of golden sands stretch all the way to Whitby. Fossils can be found nearby, and the village gives access to a woodland walk leading to the ruins of Mulgrave Castle.

It is a three mile drive to Whitby and a further ten to Robin Hood's Bay, a fascinating former haunt of smugglers where you can wander at will through a labyrinth of narrow alleyways, and low tide permits a pleasant stroll along the beach to Boggle Hole, which can also be reached by a clifftop path.

Ravenscar was once inhabited by Vikings who flew their raven flag from the cliff top; the raven flag gave its name to Raven Hall, where King George III stayed during his period of 'madness' and where, if rumours are to be believed, he fathered a child to a servant woman. Ravenscar was originally planned as a holiday resort to rival Blackpool and Scarborough. Roads were laid out and a railway station built but nobody wanted to buy property there, and eventually the developers ran out of money. At the end of the journey is Scalby Mills with its popular Sea-Life Centre, which is connected to Scarborough by a footpath and miniature railway.

MARSKE

MARSKE-BY-THE-SEA, as opposed to its modern neighbour New-Marske, is a village under the local authority of Redcar and as such is in both Yorkshire and Cleveland. It was once an area of marshy land (hence its name) and is mentioned in the Domesday Book. The citizens were once given 20 marks by the crown for their part in pillaging a Viking boat in 1180. As this old postcard shows, it was still a quiet place in the 1940s when locals gathered at the street corner to chat and the local policeman had little to do but join in the conversation.

A MODERN ROUNDABOUT now stands at the point where the policeman was standing in the old picture. The scene at first appears totally different until one examines some of the older buildings leading down to the beach at the end of the street. Nearby is Cliff House, built in the nineteenth century as a holiday residence for the Pease family. Also close by is Winkie's Castle, not really a castle but a village museum housed in the former home of a local cobbler who had a cat called Winkie. One of the museums exhibits is a two-headed lamb called 'Bill and Ben'.

SKINNINGROVE

THE YORKSHIRE VILLAGE of Skinningrove, like its near neighbours, now has a Cleveland postal address. Until the opening of the nearby ironworks in 1848 its chief industries were fishing and agriculture. This old postcard shows the village when it was at the height of its industrial past. Mining continued until 1958, and iron and steel production ceased in the 1970s. Its name is first recorded as Skynnergreve in 1301 with a number of different spellings being found in later documentation. The oldest surviving houses appear to be Nos 9-12 Stone Row, which are said to date from the 1600s.

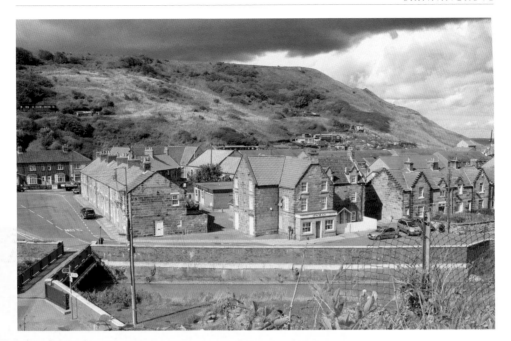

THE VILLAGE TODAY has a small population of around 450 people but enthusiastically celebrates its own history with a local history group and a popular museum, which claims to be the only UK museum to tell the story of ironstone mining. The village is also at the convergence of a number of popular public footpaths, including the Cleveland Way, so it is increasingly visited by walkers and hikers. The specific architectural style of its public buildings and houses has contributed to the area being declared a conservation area, and many of its older dwellings have been designated listed buildings.

STAITHES BANK

THIS RARE OLD photograph (right) looks like a film set from a medieval drama but was actually taken sometime in the early 1900s. In the distance a woman is washing her laundry in a wooden barrel in the street. On the left another woman in a traditional Steers bonnet is collecting water from a pump as she chats to a man in a straw hat. On the right a woman with knitting and needles in her hand converses with a younger woman dressed in a black headscarf and long apron, while a cat and chickens wander around their feet.

THE BANK TODAY is totally altered, though it still retains its historic atmosphere. All

but resident cars are banned from parking in the village and instead visitors must leave their cars in the car park at the top of the bank. Until relatively modern times the village of Staithes (known as Steers locally) remained isolated, only being visited by fishermen, smugglers and foreign vessels, including, it is said, Spanish sailors who fled the Armada when it was beaten by the British Navy. It is said that some of the older families in Staithes are descended from foreign sailors who took refuge here.

11

STAITHES FROM COWBAR

COWBAR, THOUGH A separate community, is considered part of Staithes. A steep bank runs down from the clifftop hamlet into Staithes to give motor vehicle access to the western side of the river. This old postcard shows that in former times the old track finished at the small footbridge and petered out into a footpath. Most of the buildings remain the same today, though, like the bridge which has always crossed the stream at this point, many of them have been refurbished

or enhanced. It is interesting to note that when the photograph was taken local cobles were moored under the bridge, which is still the case today.

THOUGH LITTLE ALTERED, the modern scene shows that the old road on the left has been surfaced and extended; the road now reaches beyond the bridge to the sea, giving access to the lifeboat building (centre left). A different bridge is now in place, and sea defences have been built on both sides of the river, part of which can be seen in the far distance on the right. In older times, fishing families and sailors would have inhabited practically every village house; today many of the homes have become seaside holiday lets for visitors seeking the quiet charms of this lovely little community.

13

THE
BRIDGE

THERE CAN BE few communities where the village river cannot be crossed by motor vehicles but Staithes is one such place. There are a number of pictures of various bridge structures spanning the stream, the earliest being constructed from tree branches. This particular one probably dates from around the 1930s. A number of well dressed children, one wearing a straw hat, are standing at the far end of it, perhaps watching boats tie up below. In the stream beyond the bridge are some local cobles (pronounced 'cobbles'). Their overlapping plank design has developed from that found in ancient Viking vessels.

THE MODERN STRUCTURE provides a similar vantage point for visitors to this charming place. Though none can be seen in the picture, cobles are still moored here when they are not out fishing or laying crab pots. Their style remains the same as those seen in the old photograph. In the distance it can be seen that cars now park on the new jetty where a ramp, complete with tractor, slopes down to the stream where it meets the sea. In the distance is the breakwater, which was constructed in more recent years to form a small entrance to the harbour area.

THE BARBER'S SHOP

WHEN THE DELIGHTFUL old photograph opposite was taken, John Roe's general building business was proudly advertised on the wall of the shop, which also served as barber's premises. A Steers bonnet is being worn by the woman in the centre of the picture. This form of headgear was hand made by the wives of local fishing families, generally from cotton with a stiff band at the front. It was intended as practical wear to protect the head when carrying fish baskets. Ear flaps would shelter the ears from biting winds when women helped their men to beach their fishing boats.

THE BARBER'S PREMISES today have been turned into a dwelling, standing between a larger shop premises and a public house. It is hardly recognisable except for the decorative lintels above the windows, though 'Barber's Yard', the name of the alleyway next to it, is a reminder of former days. The name 'yard' is a regional one and unlike in many other areas of the country does not mean a back yard. Instead it refers to a narrow passageway between buildings, generally, though not always, 3 feet (1 yard) across. The two canon gun barrels protecting the pavement outside are modern.

THE COD
& LOBSTER

A PUBLIC HOUSE has stood on or near this place for generations, though the sea has claimed more than one and damaged others. As can be seen from the old photograph on the right, it was once the central meeting place of the local fishing community who would sit to drink and chat, mend their nets and manufacture their hand-made crab pots. The pots, which are made from wood and cord and weighed down with anything suitable such as iron bars, stones and recycled lead pipes, are still made in exactly the same way today as they have been for centuries.

STAITHES HAS ALWAYS proved a safe haven in a storm. Today, a new pier and breakwater has been constructed to protect the community from the sometimes ferocious storms that can batter this part of the Yorkshire coastline. The modern Cod & Lobster pub still serves as a meeting place for locals, though its customers nowadays include lots of seasonal visitors. Some walkers will simply pass through when following the popular Cleveland Way footpath; others will spend a day painting or perhaps taking photographs, and some will choose to stay for a week or more in one of the little fishermen's cottages.

CAPTAIN COOK'S COTTAGE

CAPTAIN JAMES COOK, explorer and circumnavigator, is said to have spent his youth until aged sixteen working in a small Staithes grocer's shop before leaving for Whitby to take up a seafaring career. The original shop was damaged in a storm in 1767 many years after James had left the village. However, parts of it were said to have been retrieved and incorporated into the building seen in the old picture opposite. A recreation of the shop is now to be found in the fascinating Captain Cook and Staithes Heritage Centre around the corner, only a short distance away from the building.

THOUGH STORIES TELL that Cook was sacked after he stole a South Sea shilling from his employer, the truth may not be so condemning: 'taking the South Sea shilling' was simply a naval expression, meaning that a man had chosen to take up a seafaring career. Today the old building has been totally modernised and now looks completely different. The three steps leading to the door are probably also modern but the structure does at least include part of the structure of the original shop where Cook worked, and as such it undeniably deserves the right to call itself 'Captain Cook's Cottage'.

HARBOURSIDE

IN DAYS GONE by there was not very much in the way of a protective harbour wall in Staithes. Boats would be dragged upon the sands as far as away from the waves as possible. In bad winters it was not uncommon for houses at the water's edge to be washed away or substantially damaged. The Cod & Lobster was one such building. Here we see a distant view of the pub when it was a single-storey building. Today it is believed to hold the record for being the pub situated closest to the sea anywhere in the British Isles.

THIS MODERN VIEW shows that the same area is now protected by a modern sea wall stretching from the cliffs to the pub. Small boats are dragged up onto the new slipway, whilst others shelter in the harbour created by the new breakwaters. The area provided by the sea wall is also a nice place for visitors to relax and take in the sea air, or perhaps buy an ice-cream from the van which can be seen parked to the left of the picture. A careful comparison between the two pictures reveals which buildings have disappeared and which remain.

UPSTREAM

THIS OLD PHOTOGRAPH looking upstream from the harbour shows the bridge with cobles moored below. In the far distance the Staithes Viaduct, built in 1875 and demolished in 1960, can be seen. It opened for use in 1883 and carried the former coastal railway line from Whitby to Middlesbrough. Staithes railway station was closed on 5 May 1958, a victim of the railway cuts made by Dr Beecham. A number of the old station buildings remain, including the station master's house, which is now a private dwelling, and The Station Hotel, which is now called the Captain Cook Inn.

THIS MODERN
PHOTOGRAPH has been
taken from a slightly
different angle in order
to show the buildings
belonging to the hamlet of
Cowbar (high on the cliff
to the right) and Cowbar
Bank. Though both are
considered part of Staithes,
Cowbar does have a
separate identity. Cowbar
Cottages, which can be seen
at the peak of the hill, are
believed to have been built
by mine owner Mark Palmer
of Grinkle Park as housing
for his mine workers
at the former Grinkle
Ironstone mines. Today
Potash mining is carried
out nearby with deep
shafts that extend beneath
the surrounding area.

COWBAR NAB

THIS LOVELY OLD picture (right) shows Staithes fishermen and their womenfolk dragging their fishing cobles up onto the beach. The men are all dressed in trousers, woollen jumpers and some form of headgear. The women are all wearing traditional long skirts, aprons and Staithes bonnets. Most of their apparel would have been hand made. Children can be seen at the water's edge, and they too are dressed in a similar fashion to their parents. To the right is the tall, rocky outlet known as Cowbar Nab. The word *nab* is Viking in origin and, like the dialect word *neb*, it means nose.

THE DISTINCTIVE OUTLINE of Cowbar Nab today remains very much the same. Despite continual attacks by the ocean waves the solid stone outcrop has remained steadfast. A new quay area has been built at its base, together with a protective breakwater made from large boulders which connects via a walkway to the new pier structure. Just beyond here the cliffs rise even higher, reaching a height of 203 metres (666 ft) above sea level, forming the highest cliffs in England. A cliff top footpath, part of the Cleveland Way, crosses the cliffs connecting Staithes and the village of Skinningrove.

CLIFFS

THE CLIFFS IN the other direction can't match the height of Boulby but still dwarf Staithes and Roxby Beck which runs through it. The old photograph above shows how the stream opened out directly into the North Sea with little protection from the storms. Because of its position along the northern coastline it still proved a popular port of call in stormy weather, despite its isolation from inland towns in former times. Indeed it was this isolation that contributed to its reputation as the haunt of smugglers and a place where villains could hide from the authorities.

THE PIER AND breakwater (centre of picture, below) have made the waters within the harbour much calmer in modern times, though the village still sometimes takes the full blast of wintry gales. Those who visit the village in winter find the shoreline at low water a great attraction. A number of wrecks lie below nearby cliffs, some of them visible at very low water such as the SS *Clementine*, lost with its cargo of yellow bricks in 1924. Occasionally the bricks wash up on the shoreline – an unexpected find for fossil hunters looking for ammonites and belemnites.

CHANGING FASHIONS

EVEN THOUGH FEW visitors would have been seen in the village at the time this old photograph was taken, it didn't stop the locals reflecting the fashion changes to be found elsewhere. Though the women are dressed traditionally, the men-folk are not. One appears to be wearing a sea captain's uniform whilst another with a striped shirt and wide braces looks as though he may be wearing a French beret. The two youths in the picture are also dressed differently. The man in the background appears to be wearing a full formal suit complete with a stylish top hat.

TODAY IT WOULD be difficult to determine by the mode of dress alone whether a person standing on the quayside was a local or a visitor. However, these two appear to be walkers who have stopped off at Staithes whilst perhaps walking part of the 109-mile Cleveland Way. The walk opened in 1969 and quickly became one of North Yorkshire's most popular treks. The route begins inland at Helmsley and follows a spectacular scenic route passing many of North Yorkshire's historic castles and abbeys before arriving at Saltburn. It then follows onwards towards Staithes and continues beyond around the spectacular coastline.

PORT MULGRAVE

LEAVING STAITHES, THE easily missed entrance to Port Mulgrave will be found near the church at nearby Hinderwell. The narrow country lane finishes abruptly at the clifftop village where a

footpath leads down to the derelict old port. Historically a wooden jetty was used to export iron ore to the Tyne but in 1859 a stone harbour replaced it. Miners' tunnels extended to Staithes and

later in 1857 to Dale House (near Staithes) in order to bring ironstone from the Grinkle mine. During the First World War the harbour defences were destroyed by the Royal Engineers to deter any German invasion.

THESE DAYS, PORT Mulgrave attracts crowds of walkers and also serves as a venue for hoards of fossil hunters, beachcombers and bird watchers. The modern photographs show the jetty at Port Mulgrave as it looks today (top) and the actual village of Port Mulgrave (bottom) that stands nearby. What remains of the harbour can easily be reached by a steep path from the two small car parks on the cliff edge. This point also marks the spot where the road leading from Hinderwell ends abruptly and where the Cleveland Way footpath stretches in both directions towards Staithes and Runswick Bay.

RUNSWICK FROM THE SEA

THOUGH ONLY AN artist's impression, this old postcard depicts Runswick Bay from the sea and captures the ferocity of the waves that can sometimes strike this part of the North Yorkshire coastline. The cliffs here, unlike at Staithes, are very unstable, which means that parts of the village

have slid down the cliff at various times in history, often leading to the loss of dwellings and a constant realignment of the roads connecting them. The road that connects the upper part of Runswick from the rest of Runswick near the bay has also suffered from regular change due to landslips.

THE RELATIVELY NEW steep road that rises up the hillside to the left of the modern view is lined with lots of steps for intrepid walkers making the journey on foot. The old road ran a more winding route to the right of the picture but has now been all but obliterated. This panoramic photograph gives a fine view of the sweeping bay and its relationship to the upper and lower parts of the village. It also shows the enormous rocks that have been placed on the beach to form a protective barrier to protect the coast from further erosion by the waves.

CHANGES

THIS VERY OLD postcard, probably dating from the Victorian era, is one of the earliest featuring the houses of local residents as they were. It also shows a number of houses that did not survive subsequent landslips. It would seem that those closest to the shoreline fared better than those further up the hill. The worst recorded incident occurred in 1664 when villagers attending a wake realised that virtually every house was beginning to slide down the cliff. The mourners alerted

other villagers and thankfully
there were no casualties.
By morning only one house
remained: that of the dead man.

THIS VIEW ABOVE shows
virtually the same area and
the houses as they are today,
including the old Royal National
Lifeboat Institute shed. In 1978
the Runswick lifeboat put to
sea for the last time. It and its
predecessors had given 112 years
of combined service to fishermen
and mariners who found
themselves in danger in the seas
off Runswick Bay. During one
incident in 1901 the normal
crew, consisting of local seamen,
were themselves caught in a
storm, and consequently the old
men and women of the village
manned the lifeboat themselves
and successfully guided their
men safely to the shore.

THE BAY

AS CAN BE seen from this very old postcard, the bay area at the bottom of the cliff was once a very ramshackle area with roads running up various parts of the cliff side, with no sea wall to protect the village houses from the waves. In the foreground are some dilapidated farmers' barns, with an

RUNSWICK.   No 2.

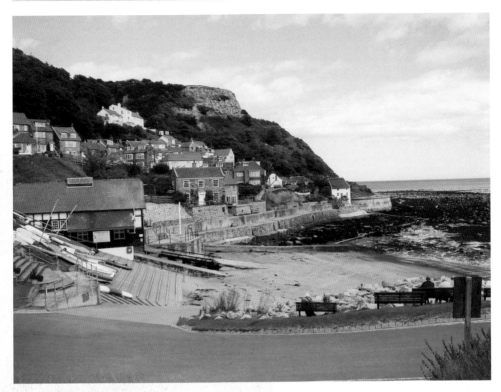

old pony trap parked nearby and a row of small fishing boats lining the sands. Some sort of roadway also appears to have existed along the edge of the bay towards the cliffs, the remnants of which can be seen here.

LANDSLIPS HAVE ERASED all of the makeshift roads and pathways between the houses on the cliff side leaving the scene as we see it today. A sea wall now protects the village houses, and those that survived previous landslips appear to be safe for the time being. In the immediate foreground can be seen the lowest part of the road which stretches up the cliff side to the rest of the village at the cliff top. Behind it is the old lifeboat shed and slipway together with another slipway nearby where boats can be pulled to safety from threatening storms.

THE
BEACH

A LATE NINETEENTH-CENTURY
account described the bay as
'...an immense inlet, called
Runswick Bay, capable of
containing several hundred
sails of ships'. The old postcard
on the right, however, shows
that around the late 1930s the
beach stretching along the bay
was attracting holidaymakers
in the summer. A number of
tents of various shapes and sizes
have been pitched along its full
length, children appear to be
enjoying their summer holidays
and a single rowing boat can be
seen in the bay. Note that the
cliff headland plunges steeply
into the sea unlike, in the picture
that follows.

FURTHER CLIFF FALLS have once more altered the layout of the village since the older picture was taken, but a row of large boulders now stretches along the bottom of the cliffs forming a protective breakwater through which a slipway has been provided to allow emergency and other vehicles to gain access to the beach. In the holiday season many more people gather on the beach, but in this picture (left) taken later in the year, only a handful of people can be seen strolling along the beach, their clothes differing greatly from fashions of the previous picture.

41

KETTLENESS

THE MAJOR PART of the village of Kettleness vanished in one fell swoop in December 1829 as a result of a major cliff fall. Most of the villagers escaped injury but one woman who refused to leave her house until the last minute became trapped halfway way down the cliff and was rescued by a small schooner anchored in the bay. Cliff Farm seen here survived. Tenant farmer William Lewis is

shown leading the shaft horse of the 'rocket cart' used to rescue shipwrecked mariners in the bay. The other villages in the picture were part of the rescue team.

WHAT REMAINS OF the village today stands at the top of a steep cliff not far from the former railway station (just left of centre). The road which once led to the seashore is now an unstable track used by hikers. There is now no sign at the cliff bottom of the small alum quay and hut which served at the terminal for a Runswick Bay to Kettleness ferry in the early 1900s. The modern picture above shows the country lane leading to Kettleness with its panoramic views over the North Sea. Opposite this is a picture of Cliff Farm as it looks today.

SANDSEND

LIKE KETTLENESS, SANDSEND, once had alum works. In 1822 the village was described erroneously as being '…situated on the face of a rocky cliff near the sea', whereas in reality it nestled within a quiet valley as shown below. The rest of the description is historically accurate: 'Here is an extensive establishment for making of alum, the property of Lord Mulgrave. There is also an abundance of terrace-stone, which is burnt and used for cement; the soil abounds lime stone. In the rocks here, and other places along the coast, black amber or jet is frequently found.'

THOUGH SOME INDUSTRY did take place on the cliffs nearby, Sandsend and its appendage East Row formed a joint community which historically was largely dependent on small time farming. Unlike other villages along this coastline, it never appears to have been a true fishing community. The modern image above shows broadly the same scene today when tourism and the renting of holiday cottages plays a large part in the village's economy. One noticeable difference is the growth in the trees in the background that now obliterates the view of the sloping hillside fields that can be seen in the previous picture.

THE PADDOCK

IN THE CENTRE of the old picture on page 44 is a small paddock or hay yard where animals could be penned up and where hay could be stacked during harvest time. This rare pencil sketch shows that same paddock at the end of the growing season when it was filled with haystacks by local smallholders. In the foreground appears to be a wattle hedge made from interwoven hazel sticks and lining the stream. In the background, the residents' cottages appear little changed from today, other than that some of them had thatched roofs.

THE SAME PLOT of land today has been fenced off to create a grassy area close to the river bank (just out of shot to the bottom left). The rest of the plot where farm wagons and haystacks once stood now forms a small, narrow road down to the cottages where local residents park their vehicles. Though this area appears in the photograph to be in an isolated rural location, it is literally only three or four minutes walk to the bridge where the main coastal road passes through Sandsend over the valley stream that empties into the North Sea.

THE BRIDGE

THOUGH ENTITLED 'THE PROMENADE', the scene below actually depicts people walking across the bridge mentioned in the previous caption, which itself leads on to the Promenade. The two-storey building seen in the mid background with a horse and cart outside looks very much like an inn but may just as well be a row of cottages. The promontory seen in the background is known

THE PROMENADE SANDSEND
FROM SANDSEND HOTEL

as Kettleness Nab. It was here that alum mining took place in former years and where in more modern times the former Whitby to Middlesbrough railway ran along the cliffs, providing spectacular sea views for its passengers.

ALTHOUGH EVERYTHING SEEN in the old picture is still present today, virtually everything has altered in appearance. The bridge has been rebuilt and realigned, and the sea wall is now concrete, having replaced the stone-built structure, which was long since washed into the sea. The slipway where the children are seen sitting in the old picture has also been obliterated by the waves, to be replaced by a version more suitable for modern usage. Even the stonework from the two-storey building appears to have been reused to build the wall that now skirts the present car park.

EAST ROW

EAST ROW WAS anciently known as Thordisa, taking its name from an ancient Saxon temple built here to the god Thor. It probably replaced another earlier Roman temple dedicated to Mars in the nearby valley, which is still named Mars Dale today. Historians believe that both temples were situated on or near the same site as a later Christian hermitage constructed in what is now Mulgrave Woods, close to the ruins of the old Mulgrave Castle. The name Thordisa was said to be still in use in 1620 when a row of cottages, 'East Row', was built here to accommodate alum miners.

THE BRIDGE SEEN opposite replaced the one seen in the old postcard after it was washed away a number of years ago following a flash flood that swept down the valley. The mill buildings to the right in both pictures were used in the manufacture of Roman cement. The cement-making process had nothing to do with the Romans, having been invented in the late 1700s. When alum mining ceased on the nearby cliffs in 1871, cement making took over. Corner and Readman's brewery formerly stood behind the white building to the left of the bridge in the modern photograph.

THE BREWERY

JOHN CORNER AND William Readman's brewery supplied local public houses in the 1890s.
It was later taken over by Scarborough and Whitby Breweries and the premises used for storage.

In 1890 John Henry Corner lived at Marine Parade, East Row (at the brewery), whilst John Corner (presumably his father) was also listed in the Whitby Trades directory in connection with the brewery, but with his home address as No. 18 Albert Road, Regent's park, London. In 1889 he was also listed in *Archaeologia Cantiana* as a member of the elite Kent Archaeological Society. William Readman's home was at No. 2 Marine Parade, Whitby.

THE BREWERY BUILDINGS today (above) have been converted to private dwellings. Though the layout remains virtually the same, a number of alterations have been made to the doors and windows. Interestingly, an old horse-mounting block of stone steps remains (to the left of the green garage door on the left) as a reminder of former days when motor transport didn't exist. To the left of the white car in the modern picture is the bridge over the stream which carries the road from Middlesbrough to Whitby, though in former times it ended here and continued towards Whitby along the beach.

MULGRAVE
CASTLE

A FOOTPATH ON the opposite side of the
bridge to the old brewery leads through
woods to Old Mulgrave Castle, shown here
(right) in an early print. A previous one,
Foss Castle, now no more than a mound,
stood nearby. The castle was originally
built by Peter de Mauley around the early
thirteenth century and was added to
and rebuilt at various times up until the
sixteenth century. The Mauley family
gave their name to Mulgrave (originally
Mauley Grave), 'grave' meaning a place of
residence rather than a burial plot. During
the Civil War a garrison of troops were
stationed there.

TODAY THE RUINS are kept in good repair, though at one time it was overgrown with sapling trees and climbing plants. These have now been removed to allow the remains to be clearly seen. A curtain wall, still intact in places, surrounds the central keep, and a stone well is still to be found in the grounds. The site, which is owned by the Mulgrave Estate, is open to the public at regular days throughout the week, except during the pheasant season in May. Access details are to be found on a board at the entrance in East Row car park.

NEW HOUSES

WHEN THESE HOMES were first built on the road leading out of the village towards Whitby, they were known as 'New Houses', a name long since gone out of use. In front of them can be seen the narrow main road skirted by a fence that hid the former coastal railway line that

ran from Whitby via West Cliff Station, towards Middlesbrough. Large steel viaducts carried the line over a number of valleys including Upgang Ravine, Raithwaite Valley, Sandsend and Staithes where in heavy winds a speed limit of 20mph was imposed or it was closed to train traffic altogether.

THE IMAGE ABOVE shows that the road in the previous picture has now been bypassed and a wider modern road follows the route of the old railway line. The road to the right sweeps around to cross over East Row Bridge and to the left continues towards Whitby. Building work has begun on the island in between the old and new roadway, where a former railway goods yard once stood. In later years, three camping coaches were situated in the same area, whilst another two were situated near the bottom of Lythe bank, at the other end of Sandsend.

SANDSEND ROAD

IN THE EARLY 1920s work began to rebuild the old Sandsend to Whitby road, which entailed moving much of the hillside that towered above it. All work was carried out using manual labour. In this old picture men with spades can be seen standing on the hillside behind the horse and skip that was used to cart away the soil. The skips were dragged up the hill to Raithwaite (pronounced Raith'et locally), where the valley was gradually being filled in to take the new road.

It is interesting to see that practically every man in the picture is wearing a cap.

THE MODERN ROADWAY stands as a testament to the hard work of those involved in making the new one. Today a long lay-by accommodates the vehicles used by hoards of visitors who park here to access the beach below (to the right). The hillside, which, like much of the coastline, had a tendency to landslips during continued spells of wet weather has been re-stabilised in recent years. In the distance can be seen the village of Sandsend. High on the hill (centre right), the top of Lythe Bank, home to Lythe village, is just out of sight behind the trees.

RAITHWAITE

HERE WE SEE the continuation of the rail used by the horse-drawn skips in the picture on page 58. The photograph below was taken on the 14 June 1922 and shows Raithwaite Valley, which had

already been largely filled in to take the new road. To the extreme right is the viaduct that carried the Whitby to Middlesbrough coastal railway. On the left, out of shot up a long driveway, stands Raithwaite Hall. In 1871 Raithwaite was described as George Ryman's country estate consisting of '137 acres, 2 roods and 20 perches' and a rental value of around £140 per annum.

ABOVE: AGAIN, WE we can see what a transformation the manual workers of the 1920s made using only basic equipment. The filled-in end of the valley now carries the main Sandsend to Whitby road, which is bordered for its entire length with a footpath for the convenience of walkers. Just above the point where the walkers are seen is the start of Whitby Golf Course, which itself stretches the full length of the road. To the left is the new road to Raithwaite with a blue board advertising a number of new one-, two- and three-bedroom cottages presently being constructed.

THE TOLL BAR

FURTHER UP THE road from the previous set of pictures was the toll bar where fees had to be paid to travel on the old road. This picture (right), taken on the first of June 1922, shows the occupier at that time buying groceries from a travelling salesman. The road to the right leads to the villages of Newholme and Dunsley. To the left is the gated road towards Whitby. As can be seen from the inset photograph of the board carrying the toll charges, fees were different depending on how many wheels and horses were pulling the cart or coach.

THIS ATMOSPHERIC PHOTOGRAPH (below) shows the toll bar house as it stands today, still set in relatively rural isolation amidst fields. The footpath leading from Sandsend to Whitby is to the left where the golf course can just

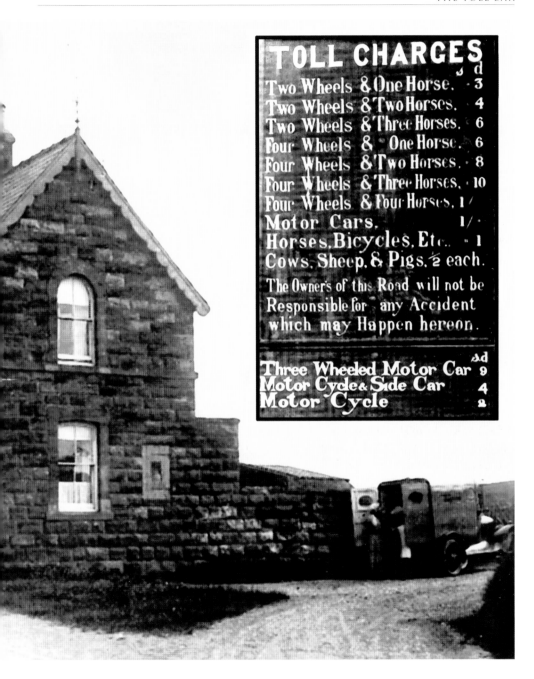

be glimpsed behind the fence. In the distance can just be seen the Sandsend Road caravan park and immediately behind it on the distant skyline, the town of Whitby. The building itself, though modernised, remains largely unchanged from the way it was almost ninety years ago, though unlike then, motor transport has taken over from the more common horses and carts of old.

ROBIN HOOD'S BAY

THE TRAVELLER HAS to go another twelve miles or so to reach the picturesque village of Robin Hood's Bay (a.k.a. 'Bay'). Like many of the villages along this coastline, Robin Hood's Bay has suffered various landslips due to the unstable nature of the cliffs. This old postcard from 1910 features part of the old village road that cannot be seen today. The worst of the landslides took

place in 1780 when King Street, the main road into the village, fell into the sea. Since that time over 200 houses have also fallen into the sea or have been destroyed by cliff falls.

THE DEEP DEPRESSION caused by the loss of the land in the area has now been landscaped and serves as a pleasant place to stroll. Seats have been installed to make the climb back up the cliff easier. Picnic tables stand nearby. The main road down to the bottom part of the village is now to the right of the picture where a car park has also been provided to cater for the large number of tourists and walkers who visit Robin Hood's Bay every year. A twenty metre high sea wall was constructed in 1975 to protect the remaining houses.

65

EROSION

BY COMPARING THIS scene with the previous modern view, one can see how the cliff has been eroded. To the left, a sweeping bay directs stormy seas directly against the village, which despite its precarious coastline has been a haunt of seafarers (including smugglers) for hundreds of years. The villagers have seen a number of prominent shipwrecks including one in 1881 when the Whitby lifeboat was unable to launch because of a blizzard and was dragged and carried overland all the way from Whitby using a hundred horses borrowed from local farmers to successfully rescue the crew of the *Visiter*.

IT'S IMPOSSIBLE TO take a modern photograph from the same position used by the photographer who took the old picture, because that part of the cliff has disappeared. The nearest point stands near this signpost pointing out the direction of the Cleveland Way. This section of the walk runs along the cliff tops from Whitby to Robin Hood's Bay and beyond. From this signpost it continues down Bay Bank before climbing again across the cliffs to Boggle Hole, Ravenscar, and eventually Scarborough. The exhilarating walk presents fantastic views of not only the coastline but also of the surrounding countryside.

BAY BANK

BAY BANK, LEADING to New Road, connects the two parts of the village. The modern part sits at the top of it, whilst 'Bay Town', as it is known, lies at the bottom. Though steep, it is the only road into the old village and, as illustrated by this old postcard (right), was regularly used by horse-drawn traffic. Steps line the steep bank side providing the only access to the lower part of the village for those on foot. To the left of the picture is one of the old gas lamps that lit the bank.

THE BUILDINGS THAT line the bank today are largely unchanged though hand rails have been provided to make the climb up and down easier for pedestrians. This, of course, is of no comfort to those people pushing prams and pushchairs, who, like the horse-drawn vehicles of old, must use the roadway. The road and path curve away to the right, passing the old Laurel Inn before winding once more into the oldest part of the village, where if legend is to be believed, mariners carried their smuggled goods from house to house via a series of tunnels and narrow passages

THE LAUREL INN

THE IMAGE OPPOSITE shows the Laurel Inn sometime around the 1930s. In 1834 Robin Hood's Bay and nearby Thorpe had ten pubs including the Laurel, whose landlord was John Matthews. The others were The Fishing boat; Royal Oak, run by John Leng; Fylingdales Inn, run by William Kell; King's Head, run by Emanuel Parkinson; Mason's Arms, run by John Thompson; New Inn, run by Thomas Robinson; the Ship, run by Tabitha Pearson; The Letters, run by Mary Avitt; and another The Letters, run by John Steel. ('Letters' signified 'board inns' and had only the name of the landlord above the door and no inn sign.)

THOUGH THE OLD railings on the bridge wall have gone, everything else remains in an ageless time warp. Even the stones used to keep the wheels of carts away from the wall on the bridge over the beck that runs through the village are still in place. Legend says that a number of tunnels ran from the little rivulet below the bridge. They connected with a maze of tunnels and passages where spirits, silk and other smuggled goods could be quickly hidden from the sight of the local customs preventative men, some of whom, it is said, turned a blind eye.

KING STREET

IN 1780, KING Street was the main road into the town until the majority of it fell into the sea in 1780. This picture shows the old village post office as it was around the 1940s, situated at the bottom section of the street, which survived. The post office also acted as the village stores and sold everything from Oxo cubes and boot blacking to tinned food and postcards. As can be seen from the sign on the side of the shop, its owner also acted as agent for the Perth Dye Works and Cleaners who probably had premises in nearby Whitby.

THE UPPER END of King Street is now truncated – as indicated by the 'dead end' traffic sign on the left – though the walk uphill proves popular as it leads to the promenade

on the new sea wall. It also connects with lots of charming tiny alleyways and steps, which are a delight to explore. Children and adults alike can be seen wending their way through this seemingly endless labyrinth of passageways during the summer months or stopping off to for a while in one of the numerous tea rooms and small shops that are to be found in the village.

BACK STREETS

THE BACK STREETS of Robin Hood's Bay are really no more than pedestrian pathways, though, as the old picture shows, in some of the wider ones a footpath was laid down the centre to make walking easier on the cobbled surface used by donkey- or horse-drawn carts. When this photograph was taken, the majority of the population of the village would have been local seafarers and their families but today many of the homes serve as retirement cottages or holiday homes for people who choose to spend their recreational time by the sea.

DESPITE THE NARROWNESS of some of these alleyways (or 'yards' as they are better known locally), plants, small trees, shrubs and window boxes abound. In summer when the sun beats down, visitors could be forgiven for imagining that they were in some Mediterranean hideaway rather than a village on the north east coast of Yorkshire. The evocative street names such as Sunny Place, The Openings, Way Foot, The Bolts, Tommy Baxter Street and Flag Staff Steps all add to the magical feel of this extraordinary old village where contraband tea, gin, spirits and tobacco were once smuggled into inland Yorkshire.

THE DOCK

THE OPEN AREA known as The Dock marks the end of King Street and New Road. It forms a central meeting point and has been used for gatherings and events for decades. In this picture we see a group of foxhounds, probably the Staintondale Hunt. The old post office on King Street stands behind them. Staintondale is a nearby hamlet within hiking distance of Robin Hood's Bay, being slightly inland from Ravenscar. It was once owned by the Knights Hospitallers. They were granted the dale by 'Henry, the son of Ralph' at the time of King Stephen and surrendered it in 1541.

VISITORS ARE SURPRISED to find that The Dock is not a conventional jetty where ships tie up, though a slipway does run down directly into the sea at high tide, and to the

beach when the tide is out. Instead it forms a kind of village square where people arrange to meet, gather to sit and chat or simply to wait for the tide to go out. Shops and pubs stand nearby. The Old Coastguard station at the top of the slipway, close to where the Robin Hood's Bay Lifeboat was kept, has been converted into a visitor centre.

SITTING AROUND

SITTING AROUND ON The Dock has long been a regular pastime. In this old photograph, ageing local seafarers are seen sitting down for a chat. It is said that the majority of the men in the photograph were at least eighty years old and the oldest was ninety-three. It is interesting to see the variety of headgear worn by the old residents. One wears a straw hat, another a low top hat, two have flat caps, one wears a kind of beret and the other a trilby-type hat with its crown pushed out.

THE SCENE BELOW is one that all the old men would recognise as they looked towards the other side of The Dock from their bench. (Note how their bench had been purposely built with one tall leg and one short one to take account of the sloping ground.) Clothing today is just as varied, though the use of hats has largely gone out of fashion. Unlike in days of old, those sitting down are virtually all visitors. The Bay Hotel, which has windows that look directly out over the bay, was extended in 1920 to take in former stables.

LIFEBOAT

THIS PHOTOGRAPH SHOWING the launching of Robin Hood's Bay RNLI rowing lifeboat must have been taken shortly before it was decommissioned in 1931. Though villages always had their own rescue boat on hand, the Royal National Lifeboat Institution provided the *Ephraim and*

Hannah Fox lifeboat for the villagers' use in 1881 after the rescue of the *Visiter* described earlier. It was superseded by the *Mary Ann Lockwood* in 1902. The coastguard station was also situated close to the top of the slipway and was still there in 1931 when the motorised lifeboat at Whitby took over responsibility for maritime incidents.

THE OLD COASTGUARD station, seen here, is now a visitor centre. To its left is situated the slipway where the lifeboat would be launched. The set of steps climbing up the hillside lead to the Quarterdeck, a promenade that forms part of the modern sea defences. The group of people in the picture are typical of those taking part in the eclectic pastimes offered by Robin Hood's Bay: one is in a wetsuit, another carries a shrimp net and a child on the right rests with a bucket and spade. On the left is an advertising board for ghost walks.

COASTGUARD

HERE WE SEE the old coastguard in former times. The picture is undated but was possibly taken after the end of the Second World War when fishing boats were still being dragged up the slipway and stored in the street. The photograph is particularly interesting because it shows

a local coble boat out of the sea with its sail fully hoisted. Interestingly, it also shows a weighing machine near the shop on the right. These machines were once common outside of shops and chemists. People could instantly obtain their weight (shown on a large clock-like dial) by placing a penny in a slot.

ABOVE IS ANOTHER view of the same scene today. Boats of a different kind are still to be found here, though they are now dragged away from the main part of the road, which as a sign of the times is edged with yellow no-parking lines. The same set of steps can be seen to the right of the old coastguard station. They form part of the Cleveland Way footpath via a clifftop footpath, which gives spectacular views on the way to Boggle Hole. An alternate route to the old mill is via the slipway to the beach at low tide.

NEW ROAD

NEW ROAD IS seen opposite on an old art postcard from a viewpoint on the steps leading up the side of the coastguard station. Few people are on the street. Boats are still moored on the street below and smoke can be seen coming from the chimneys of the houses which at that time would all have had coal or wood-burning fires. Fuel was often collected from the beach in the form of driftwood and coal washed from passing collier ships. These regularly passed the village on their way to London from the northern coal mines.

NEAT, CLEAN AND brightly-painted buildings line the street today, which in essence is little different from over a hundred years ago. Interestingly, even at that time the village attracted visitors and the street contained a number of apartments for visitors. Though addresses aren't given, an 1890 street directory lists nineteen women who were seaside landladies with apartments catering for visitors. At that time Robin Hood's Bay had its own railway station (a Mr Tindal Bowman was the station master). Another prominent resident at that time was Joseph Cooper who served as chief officer at the village coastguard station.

LOOKING BACK

WALKERS LEAVING ROBIN Hood's Bay can look back over the village from their high vantage point on the clifftop. Constant erosion means that the direction of the footpath has altered over the years. The village too has changed and developed as can be seen by carefully comparing the outlines of the roofs and buildings in this old view of Bay Town and the one in the modern picture. In this particular view the sea has receded to reveal the scaur where periwinkles (known locally as winkles or 'cuvins') were once gathered in great numbers for sale to fish merchants.

WALKERS ON THE Cleveland Way footpath to Boggle Hole can see the full extent of the village and how the lower portion is clearly separated from the newer village at the top of Bay Bank. Though the growth of trees has largely obliterated the view of some of the houses from the clifftops, the outlook over the sea and surrounding countryside is spectacular. The footpath is well maintained, though the muddy structures of the cliffs that are responsible for much of the erosion can clearly be seen here. To the bottom right of the modern image is the promenade area known as the Quarterdeck.

BOGGLE HOLE

BOGGLE HOLE MILL is reached by a clifftop footpath or by beach at low tide from Robin Hood's Bay. It is also accessible by car from the Whitby to Scarborough road at Pond Hill. The old water mill sits by a stream that opens out into the sea close by. Boggle (or boggart) comes from local legend and means malevolent goblin. In this case one was said to haunt the cove and attack trespassers. The

The Mill, Robin Hood's Bay

story was probably put about by smugglers who once used the inlet to bring in their contraband from ships anchored in the bay.

THE BUILDING TODAY has been extended and now serves as a youth hostel and public café. It is a popular stop for walkers on the Cleveland Way, which continues onto Stoupe Beck and then along the old railway line track to Ravenscar. The line between Whitby and Scarborough opened in 1885 and provided spectacular views of the coastal scenery. It was closed in 1965 under the notorious 'Beeching Cuts'. Those staying at the youth hostel generally arrive today on foot, with the prospect of enjoying fabulous clifftop and beach walks or hunting for Jurassic fossils, which abound in the area.

RAVENSCAR

RAVENSCAR IS BARELY a village, though it was meant to be a major holiday town to rival Blackpool and other coastal resorts. The old map on the right shows the plan of its first phase with plots and features clearly laid out. Funicular railways were meant to join the cliff top to the beach below. A railway station (ringed) was built to bring the thousands of expected visitors. Unfortunately, few investors could be found to buy into the dream of 'Royal Ravenscar', which was based on the fact that 'mad' King George stayed at Raven Hall during his period of illness in the late 1700s.

AS THE PICTURE above shows, the town square and railway station ringed in the previous picture are virtually the only buildings to be found in this part of the proposed town centre. The carefully laid out streets (all named) complete with a fully functioning sewer system are now lost under the vegetation of years and will certainly pose a mystery to any archaeologists of the distant future who should stumble upon them. The speculators who were responsible for changing the area's name from Peak to Ravenscar abandoned their dream in 1913 having sold less than a dozen houses.

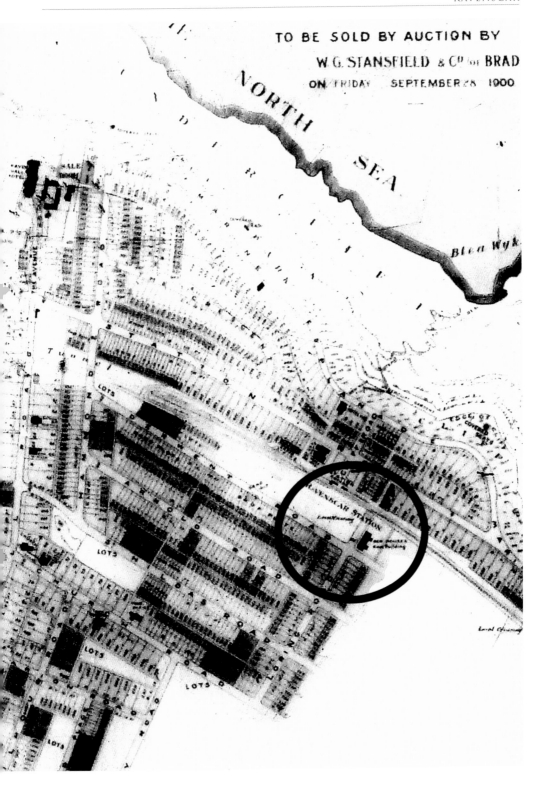

TO BE SOLD BY AUCTION BY

W. G. STANSFIELD & Cᴰ ᴼꜰ BRAD

ON FRIDAY SEPTEMBER 28 1900

RAVENSCAR STATION

PEAK STATION, AS it was then known, was opened in July 1885 and formed the highest point
of the Scarborough & Whitby Railway, being reached by a steep climb in both directions. It
was re-named Ravenscar on the first of October 1897 and fell foul of the Dr Beeching cuts in

the 1960s, closing on 8 March 1965. This was not the only destructive event in its history: the wooden waiting room was blown away in a storm during the 1800s. During the 1960s a camping coach made from a railway carriage provided a popular holiday home here.

THE RAILWAY PLATFORM is barely recognisable today, having gradually been taken over by nature. It is, however, kept neat and tidy and a picnic table now stands where the steam trains once whistled past. The track forms a popular hiking and cycle path, which has been described as one of the foremost cycle routes in the UK, because of its easy navigability and spectacular views. The station is often missed by motorists because of its location, so those wishing to find the centre of 'The Town That Never Was' must turn right at the gates to Raven Hall.

SCALBY MILLS

OUR JOURNEY ENDS at Scalby Mills (a coastal extension of the village of Scalby further inland). Like many of the villages on this coastline its residents are split between those at the top of the cliff and those down below. The Scalby Mills Hotel, however, personifies Scalby Mills to most local people as it has stood here for generations. The area had a mill belonging to the Crown as early as 1164 and at a later date, three other mills are recorded, one being on Langdale Beck. The gated road is now open, allowing access to the sea life centre nearby.

UGH – SCALBY MILLS

A BRIDGE NOW crosses the beck nearby the hotel whereas in earlier times visitors used a waste pipe to access the sands. The beach area at Scalby Mills has recently become famous because of a number of dinosaur footprints found in the rocks nearby and attracts increasing numbers of tourists and geologists. The area has always been popular with fossil hunters and now forms part of the 'Dinosaur Coast'. The adjacent sea life centre, Scarborough Sea Life and Marine Sanctuary, can be reached from Scarborough by road or by a miniature train run by the North Bay Railway Company.

Other titles published by The History Press

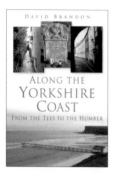

Along the Yorkshire Coast: From the Tees to the Humber
DAVID BRANDON

This book is a unique record of a journey along the beautiful and often dramatic Yorkshire coastline, tracing the region's diverse industry, the history of its settlements, seaside resorts and fishing quays, and reflecting upon the different uses to which man has put the resources where sea and land meet. With a blend of photographs, fact, folklore and social history, David Brandon offers a fascinating and evocative look the county's local history, and should capture the imagination of anyone who knows the places that are featured.

978 0 7524 5732 1

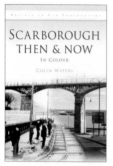

Scarborough Then & Now
COLIN WATERS

This fascinating volume captures the essence of the town and its people over the decades in a series of photographic pairings which record some of Scarborough's lost landmarks, such as the North Bay Promenade Pier, the arch at Newborough Bar and the town's two swimming pools. Illustrated throughout with carefully selected pictures and photographs of Scarborough's past and modern colour photographs of the same scenes today, this book will delight any lover of Scarborough and its history.

978 0 7524 6299 8S

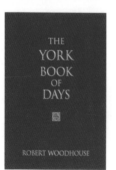

The York Book of Days
ROBERT WOODHOUSE

Taking you through the year day by day, *The York Book of Days* contains a quirky, eccentric, amusing or important event or fact from different periods of history, many of which had a major impact on the religious and political history of England as a whole. Ideal for dipping into, this addictive little book will keep you entertained and informed. Featuring hundreds of snippets of information gleaned from the vaults of York's archives, it will delight residents and visitors alike.

978 0 7524 6045 1

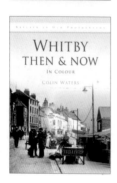

Whitby Then & Now
COLIN WATERS

Social historian Colin Waters has carefully selected a wide variety of captivating archive images, ranging from scenes of old narrow streets and local people to nostalgic harbour views and the town's majestic abbey. Each old picture is complimented with a modern colour photograph and a detailed caption providing fascinating insights into the history of this charming town. This absorbing book will be of interest to all lovers of nostalgia and a welcome addition to the bookshelf of every lover of Whitby and its historic past.

978 0 7524 6315 5

Visit our website and discover thousands of other History Press books.

www.thehistorypress.co.uk